W9-BNT-813

A SPECTATOR'S GUIDE TO

Figure Skating

A SPECTATOR'S GUIDE TO
Figure Skating

DEBBI WILKES

Trafalgar Square Publishing

First published in the United States of America in 1998 by
Trafalgar Square Publishing, North Pomfret, Vermont 05053

First published in Canada in 1997 by Key Porter Books, Toronto, Ontario M5E 1R2

Printed in Canada

ISBN: 1-57076-106-X

Library of Congress Catalog Card Number: 97-61778

Design: Leah Gryfe
Electronic formatting: Heidi Palfrey

98 99 00 01 6 5 4 3 2 1

Contents

Introduction

If you can't tell a Lutz from a klutz, this is the book for you. Let me tell you about yourself. You are a lover of figure skating, but probably not a serious skater. If you're older than twenty-five, your skating love affair probably began in February 1988 when the Olympic torch was lit in Calgary. At that very moment, figure skating was about to explode and take off in new directions, carrying you along with it.

Back then in Calgary, sitting in the sidelines at the Saddledome, those of us who were already in love with skating had no idea the rest of the world was about to discover this intoxicating, romantic, often brutal and death-defying sport. New-found fans like you, many of whom had never even been in a pair of figure skates, were suddenly expounding on the virtues of the perfect triple Axel! It was bound to happen.

It's a culture that is both fascinating and compelling, and now, with promises of riches and rewards to the precious few who excel at it, the stakes have soared beyond titles and technique. Funny, but the fact that some of the greatest champions have not been the greatest skaters hasn't hurt the sport a bit. We've become addicted to the sparkling personalities and how they react to the brutality of a sport that is known for eating its young. It's a roller coaster ride, with the demands often unrealistic one day and the expectations downright hopeless another. Take one unknown skater, hang a medal around his neck and watch the metamorphosis begin.

This is exciting stuff! Every year the experts believe we've reached the end of the road. After all, how many times can a skater turn around in the air without amputating her lower leg on landing? Yet each year, these experts leave the World Championships smiling and shaking their heads in breathless disbelief, not only at the virtuoso technical skills the skaters have displayed, but also at the artistic courage they've shown. We've made our skaters heroes and they've repaid their debts with dedication, vision and heart.

Even for the knowledgeable fan, watching the dizzying array of "tricks" can be a mind-boggling experience. What is an Axel anyway? Everybody has an opinion about what makes one jump better than another, and if you want to share this insider knowledge about skating, you need to get busy and do some homework yourself. It's not important to know how to *do* a triple Axel (that's something you can't learn from any book), but it is important to know what one looks like.

How to Use This Book

In the following pages, my goal is to help you understand exactly what you're watching on television or from the stands. You'll learn how to distinguish one jump from another, how to recognize a top-notch spin and what to look for in quality pair skating. It's just like becoming a good skater. It takes time and patience and *practice*.

My analysis will examine the most common elements in singles and pairs. These moves are the foundation of a skater's alphabet and are how he learns to express himself through skating. For the viewer, the step-by-step breakdowns of these elements and what makes them distinctive are the nuggets of technical insight every fan needs to have to be able to "talk" skating, too.

I may take a few shortcuts, not to confuse you but to help you focus on the most important factors for identification. In these basic elements, certain stages are identical. For example, every jump lands on the same edge, and every standard spin begins from the same edge. Within each section, I'll remind you about these similarities and then I'll emphasize their differences.

For the purposes of this book, I will describe jumps and spins that turn in a *counterclockwise direction*. (Imagine that you are looking down at the ice surface from the roof of the arena.) Unlike ballet dancers, skaters develop their sense of rotation in only one direction. If a skater is left-handed, it may feel more natural for him to spin clockwise, but whatever a skater's individual preference, his jumps and spins will usually rotate the same way.

A word of warning. My opinions will be front and center, and although I hold to them, I recommend that you use them as a reference point. You may find that our tastes are opposite or that you prefer a different look. Why should we be any different from the individuals sitting at the judges' table?

The Basics

Skating only looks complicated. Every trick is based on six major jumps and four basic spins. Pair skaters and dancers use the same fundamental moves. Since a competitor's repertoire is by no means limited to these elements, keep in mind that this is just the foundation.

To begin, let's talk generally about the common factors in all good technical skating, singles, pairs or dance.

Look for *speed* and how quickly the skater moves over the ice. For instance, a jump that covers a short distance is inferior to one that spreads itself over a greater area. Similarly, a program that uses only half the ice or constantly repeats the same pattern with elements in the same spots is easier to perform than one that covers the whole ice surface. Everything skaters do should highlight their ability to glide with ease and flow.

Flow is more difficult to define than speed. When you watch some skaters, they appear to move effortlessly across the ice. Others have to work extra hard, huffing and puffing to reach the same speed and distance. The first skater has flow, the second skater looks like he's skating on golf cleats.

Form, or style, is also important. It includes such things as pleasing body line, stretched legs, pointed toes and good posture, all packaged in fit and toned bodies. These days skaters with some of the worst-looking styles are making it to the top just because they can do triple jumps. This kind of jumping ability deserves to be rewarded, but not to the exclusion of good spins, footwork and choreography. These latter require a finesse and control that these new-wave jumpers often lack.

During a spin, when the skater's innate sense of balance is tested against outside forces such as speed and rotation, the phenomenon of *control* comes into play. Most skaters are exciting to watch, but if you have to cover your eyes for fear their next move will paste them into the boards, they are not skating with control. All movement should appear comfortable and confident no matter how difficult the trick.

Along with speed and flow, competitors skating *deep curving edges* that twist and wind around the ice are considered better technicians than those who continually move in straight lines on two feet. It's much harder to stay on balance on one foot while skating on a curve. Try it and you'll see what I mean! The more difficult the maneuver, the more likely the skater will lose control, either by falling or by putting the other foot down to restore his equilibrium.

Finally, skaters must have *power, strength* and *endurance.* These are the combined abilities that allow the competitor to deliver consistently strong and clean elements for the duration of a performance. In short, the skater must be able to resist the effects of the number-one killer—fatigue.

As you study the basic elements, you'll gain an even greater respect for the athletes who try to achieve them. Stick with it. At first your identifications will mostly be guesses, but as your eye develops, you'll begin to see that every element has its own set of characteristics—for example, the way a jump looks during the early preparation, or where it's set up on the ice. If you're still lost on occasion, don't despair! Even old gypsies like me get them wrong sometimes.

The Jumps: Getting the Facts

Skaters, judges and fans consider jumps the hardest elements and therefore the most important. All other tricks, spins, field moves and footwork must have the same high speed, complexity and ice coverage as jumps, but because the skater moves through the air free of the ice during jumps, they provide an additional force to conquer.

The ability to become a good jumper is based on several things: body type, jumping technique, power and nerve. You've probably already noticed the best jumpers have small bodies that are perfectly proportioned. (Height is a definite disadvantage—too much body to control!) There is also a feeling shared by all those great jumpers. They love to be up in the air, even if it's just for a fraction of a second.

As a fan of jumps, it's kind of scary to try to test your perceptions with such split-second moves, but it should help you to know there are some basic guidelines to follow. You might think there are thousands of jumps you'll need to learn to recognize, but you can relax. The magic number is only six.

What to look for

A good jump will have speed, height, distance, rotation and control.

On takeoff, a skater's first objective is to have enough *speed* to power the jump. The body should be well balanced and prepared to handle the force from the takeoff. The preparation before the jump should flow confidently and without hesitation into a smooth takeoff.

At this point, the goal is to lift the jump high enough to complete the rotation. Without *height*, no matter how fast the rotation in the air, the jump will look like a hiccup, appearing as if it takes off and lands in the same place without having traveled any *distance* across the ice.

Once airborne, the body position changes to accommodate the *rotation*, the body remaining tightly tucked and controlled for multiple rotations and more loosely positioned for simpler jumps.

As the landing approaches, the skater will slow down the rotation by "opening up," or loosening, the arms and legs, moving them away from the rest of the body. This is the moment in the jump when all the evidence of good technique can shine through. When done well, the landing will have as much speed as the takeoff. The longer the skater can hold the landing position, the greater the *control*, and the better the jump.

Stages in jumping

All jumps have four stages: *preparation*, the way a skater sets the jump up on the ice; *takeoff*, the method used to jump; *flight*, the body's position in the air; and *landing*, how the skater settles back on the ice. Every stage depends on the one before. If the skater loses her balance on the takeoff, she's not likely to land well. However, a few skaters have demonstrated a preternatural ability to land on their feet, having taken off almost upside down. This may look awkward, but the jump gets done without a fall.

Once they're up in the air, the six common multirotational jumps are basically the same, and all land on the same backward outside edge.

Words such as *single*, *double*, *triple* or *quad* (short for *quadruple*) refer to the number of rotations performed during a jump. Obviously, the greater the number of rotations, the more difficult the jump, but even for a skater who has mastered all six triples, some jumps are harder than others. Top skaters regularly feel a certain jump is their nemesis. For instance, World champion Kurt Browning hated the triple Lutz and only included it in his performance after being pressured to do so. Olympic gold medalist Kristi Yamaguchi often found the simple triple Salchow was the only mistake in her otherwise perfect program.

Identifying jumps

So what sets them apart? Watch the takeoff.

Every jump is defined at takeoff by the answers to the following three questions.

1. What is the *direction* of movement at takeoff?

Immediately before the skater launches into the air, is she gliding forward or backward?

2. Which *edge* is used during the takeoff, the outside or inside one?

Hold the skating boot upside down and look closely along the bottom of the skate blade from heel to toe. See how the blade is high on the sides with a U-shaped valley in the middle? These high, sharp sides are the edges, the parts of the blade that actually carve into the ice. With speed, when the skater leans over the outside of the foot, he is skating on the outside edge. When he leans the other way over the instep, he is skating on an inside edge.

3. Is a *toe pick* used to take off?

To whittle down the confusion even further, the six major jumps fall into two categories: *edge jumps*, which are those that do *not* use the toe pick on takeoff, such as the Axel, the Salchow and the loop, and *toe jumps*, those that *do* use the toe pick, such as the toe loop, the flip and the Lutz.

If you can answer these three questions, you can identify every jump. Now, let's try!

The Loop
(an edge jump)

1. Direction of takeoff? Backward.
2. Type of edge? Outside.
3. Is the toe pick used? No, this is an edge jump.

The first edge jump, the loop, is developed from the compulsory figure by the same name. Its movement in the air is the root position for the body's posture and balance in all multirotation jumps. Every other jump is unique on its takeoff, then evolves into the loop once in flight. More simply, some special movement is added to the beginning of the loop to give each jump its own identity. Once the skater learns this loop feeling and can relate it to the other triples, everything starts to make sense. Instead of thinking that every jump relies on a different set of techniques, you begin to see just how closely related the jumps really are; for instance, the toe loop jump is just a loop jump with a toe pick used on takeoff.

Preparation and Takeoff

What sets the loop apart from other jumps is its simplicity. The takeoff and landing are skated on the same foot, and because it's an edge jump, you don't have to check for that quick toe pick.

In the early stages, the preparation looks exactly like the first step in a long backward crosscut. At this point, the skater usually glides on two feet with the right arm back and the left arm in front. Just as in the Sal takeoff, the body appears to be readying itself for flight. Most of the weight is over the right foot and when the right knee begins to bend to spring, the left foot stays on the ice and pulls the rest of the body into the rotation. Once airborne, the left leg winds itself around the front of the right leg with both feet together in a crossed position.

THE LOOP OVERVIEW

This edge jump gives a skater the root position for jumps and the basic feeling of moving through the air, upon which he will build all other jumps. The skater starts by stepping onto a deeply bent right leg that is skating on a back outside edge (2). He then springs into the air (3). Unlike other takeoffs, his free leg remains in front (4), with feet crossed during flight (5 and 6—the basic position during rotation). Takeoff and landing are skated on the same foot.

LOOP DETAILS

The body leans to the outside of the right foot, so that the skater is skating on an outside edge. The skater shifts the balance on the right foot by rocking forward on the blade to a point just behind the toe pick. The left free foot moves to cross over the takeoff foot.

The toe pick of the right foot is the first part of the blade to touch the ice on the landing. The left foot kicks forward to open up the body and stop the rotation.

The landing is all about aesthetics! The back is erect and the head is up. The arms and hands are extended, right down to the fingertips, and are carried at a level between the waist and the shoulders.

Bad

- *Turning too much on the ice* during the takeoff. This is caused by curling the entry edge too deeply or by turning the shoulders too soon.
- *Wrapping the left leg* too tightly around the right with the left foot carried too high up the right leg. This strains the body's ability to stop the rotation and get comfortably into the landing. It also torques the body into awkward positions during flight.

Good

- *In-flight position should be erect,* arms pulled in close to the body, legs and feet crossed together, toes pointed.
- *Left free leg should be either stretched behind or moving into that position by the time the skater lands.* If it's still in front at the landing, it indicates the rotation has just been squeaked out.

History

- The loop is also called the Rittberger.
- The first triple loop was completed in 1952 when American Dick Button landed it in competition. Dick was also the originator of the "triple-double," a jump sequence with three double loop jumps done one after the other.
- A legal combination has no turn or step between jumps and, since almost all triples land on the same backward outside edge, the second jump *must* begin on that same back outside edge. This gives you only two possibilities: the triple loop jump and the loop's sister, the triple toe loop.

The Axel
(an edge jump)

1. Direction of takeoff? Forward.
2. Type of edge? Outside.
3. Is the toe pick used? No, this is an edge jump.

The "A-word," as skaters respectfully call the Axel, is considered the most difficult of all the triples, but it's the easiest for the fan to identify because it's the only major jump with a forward takeoff. Many skaters feel that because of the forward entry, they have less control and more potential for problems. Although the Axel is called a single jump, it's actually one and a half rotations. Similarly, the triple Axel is three and a half rotations.

Preparation and Takeoff

Positioning the triple Axel on the ice requires intense concentration. Not only is the jump fast and high, but a good one covers a great distance. If the skater begins a jump too near a corner or against the boards, he won't have enough room to land; it's important for the skater to pay attention to his radar and keep track of available space.

As I have already mentioned, most skaters rotate left to right in a counterclockwise direction. To demonstrate exactly what it looks like turning the other way, let's flip the Axel, for this one jump only, so that it will rotate right to left in a clockwise direction.

The regular setup for the Axel is to glide long enough on a left back outside edge to get into a perfectly balanced posture that will carry through the jump. Looking for the forward entry can be a confusing moment for a fan. After the long wait going backward, the skater will surprise you by suddenly stepping forward and pushing powerfully on to the right foot, bending the right knee like a huge spring and reaching far behind with the left leg and with both arms. At the exact moment the right knee springs to jump, two critical things must happen. First, the skater must roll her

Remember, we've changed the direction of this jump from counterclockwise to clockwise. It's the difference between watching an Axel done by Elvis Stojko, who jumps left to right, and one skated by Todd Eldredge, who jumps right to left.

THE AXEL OVERVIEW

Gliding backward (1), the skater prepares for takeoff and steps forward (2). He begins the jumping action by thrusting his arms and legs in front (4). After half a rotation in midair (5), he shifts his balance from right foot to left foot as for the loop jump position. He then opens up his body (6) in preparation for landing.

AXEL DETAILS

To begin the takeoff, the skater pushes powerfully from backward to forward as she steps from a left back outside edge to a right forward outside edge. This action sets up the split-second timing for launching the body into the air.

Takeoff is the moment that separates the Axel from all other jumps because the Axel is the only jump with a forward takeoff. Here the skater rolls up on to the right toe pick to spring into the air, still moving in a forward direction. The left leg kicks in front to help get the jump up to its full height. More height means more time for rotation.

Once the rotation begins, the weight is transferred in midair from right to left, allowing the feet to cross and putting the body into a tighter position to increase the speed of rotation. The best singles, doubles and triples take basically the same amount of time to complete. In triple jumps, the rotation just happens more quickly.

balance up to the right toe and press off it while leaping into the air. Then she has to throw her arms and left leg in front to take the jump up to its fullest height.

Bad

- *Too little rotation* due to poor takeoff action. The arms and the free leg do not complete the full "kicking-through" action.
- *Skidding the takeoff.* This results from bad balance or from not pushing into the air from the forward part of the blade. In this case, the skater is actually starting the rotation on the ice.

Good

- *Large distance covered* across the ice.
- *Rotation complete* while still at the full height of the jump; the jump appears to float to the ice on the landing.

History

- The Axel takeoff is the same as the waltz jump's, the first half-rotation jump a beginner will learn. Unlike the Axel, which is performed in "tuck" position, the waltz jump is made with the legs split in the air. Today, the waltz jump is used for warming up.
- Double and triple versions of the Axel are based on the single Axel (one and a half rotations), invented by Norwegian speed skater and figure skater Axel Paulsen.
- The earliest official performance of the single Axel occurred during the first major international figure-skating competition, in Vienna in 1882, when Paulsen finished third and skated the Axel as a figure.
- In the early 1920s, Sonja Henie was the first woman to complete the Axel.
- The double Axel (two and a half rotations) was introduced by American Dick Button in 1947.
- Canadian Vern Taylor executed the first triple Axel during the 1978 World Championships in Ottawa, Canada.
- Japanese champion Midori Ito made history when she successfully performed a triple Axel at the World Championships in 1989, the first woman to do so.

The Salchow
(an edge jump)

1. Direction of takeoff? Backward.
2. Type of edge? Inside.
3. Is the toe pick used? No, this is an edge jump.

Considered the easiest of the big jumps, the Salchow, or the Sal as skaters call it, is the first full-rotation jump learned by beginners.

Preparation and Takeoff

This can be tricky, not because the Salchow is such a hard jump, but because its natural action is quick and unexpected. It can appear anywhere: in jump sequences, out of footwork and with weird entrances.

The standard approach is off a left forward outside three, turning to a left back inside edge. While holding that edge for several seconds and waiting for the best moment to jump, the skater looks like she is gathering her body together. First she stretches her arms and legs out and then pulls them in tightly with one strong movement. The right leg is behind during the three-turn and then begins to swing around the side of the body from behind to in front, signaling to the skating knee that it's time to spring. During the "gathering" seconds, some skaters may bounce the skating knee slightly, bending and straightening in a slow rhythm that explodes as the body takes flight.

In the air, the skater must adjust her balance: Having taken off on the left foot, she must land on the right. Although this movement is almost imperceptible to the nonskater, when done well, the viewer will feel a certain confidence in the skater. The skater appears to land effortlessly by simply reaching for the ice. However, if the skater is late adjusting her balance, the jump looks off center.

THE SALCHOW OVERVIEW

The skater glides on the left back inside edge (1). The right free leg then swings around the body from behind to in front (2). As the right foot passes in front of the left, the jump lifts into the air (3) and starts to rotate (4). As in the Axel, the skater shifts his weight from left to right (5) during rotation in the basic loop jump position, then settles onto the right back outside landing edge (6 and 7).

SALCHOW DETAILS

The Salchow is an edge jump and uses no toe pick. The impetus for the jump comes from swinging the right foot in a circular pattern around the takeoff foot.

As the right foot sharply crosses in front, the left leg and foot spring to jump. The curved pattern being skated on the ice and the circular action of the right leg create the rotation. The stronger the action of the right free foot on the takeoff, the greater the potential for rotation.

A perfectly landed Salchow has the left leg and foot stretched behind the right and held slightly above the ice, toe and knee turned out. The right landing knee is bent, like a huge spring, to absorb the shock of the landing.

Bad

- *Scratchy takeoff.* This is caused by balancing so far forward on the blade that the ice is gouged out by the toe picks.
- *Incorrect lean.* As the jump approaches the takeoff, the shoulders should be level. If the body is leaning with the left shoulder down, the timing of the jump is rushed, which results in poor height and rotation.

Good

- *Large, wide arc.* The jump shape across the ice from takeoff through to landing makes the shape of a large, flowing curve.
- *Open rotation.* Jumps that spin quickly have less height than those that float with looser rotation.

History

- The single Salchow was invented by Ulrich Salchow, Swedish World champion from 1901 to 1905, and 1907 to 1911, and Olympic champion in 1908.
- At the 1955 World Championships, American Ronnie Robertson was third in figures, but with an incredible free skate, which included the first triple Salchow, he won the free and finished with a silver medal.
- Canadian World champion Petra Burka was the first woman to perform the triple Salchow. She did so at the World Championships in 1965, where she won the world title.
- In pair skating, American and World champions Tai Babilonia and Randy Gardner were the first team to show the world a throw triple Salchow.

The Toe Loop
(a toe jump)

1. Direction of takeoff? Backward.
2. Type of edge? Outside.
3. Is the toe pick used? Yes, this is a toe jump.

Most people feel the toe loop is the easiest triple. (Remember, everything's relative.) At first, the viewer will be able to tell that it's a toe jump but will often confuse the toe loop with the flip: both are toe jumps with backward entries, but the two jumps have different takeoff edges. Notice the similarities between the toe loop and its close relative, the loop.

Preparation and Takeoff

The toe loop is another jump that usually travels lengthwise, end to end, on the ice surface. Before the skater turns backward, the setup can look similar to the flip's, with the skater posing forward for several seconds to take a breath and think. The entry may be set up in many different ways and from various steps, but whatever the entry, the takeoff is always from the right backward outside edge with a quickly placed left toe pick stabbing into the ice. The body weight begins to transfer onto the left foot so the action of the right leg can lift the jump up to its height.

Bad

- *Placing the toe pick incorrectly.* This fails to let the jump lift high enough.
- *"Cheating" the landing.* This involves an incomplete rotation. The skater lands forward and turns the last half rotation on the ice instead of in the air.

Good

- *More attention paid to height than to rotation.* This technique should clearly show the jump gets to its height before it spins—up first, then around.

TOE LOOP OVERVIEW

The glide on the right back outside edge of the takeoff is very short in the toe loop and is accented by the sudden "picking" of the left toe (2). The pick acts the way the pole does for a pole vaulter. The skater climbs over the picking foot and up into the air (3). Once in flight, the feet cross in the basic loop jump position (4) until the rotation is complete (5) and the skater reaches for the ice (6) to land.

TOE LOOP DETAILS

The left foot reaches behind the right foot and the left toe stabs into the ice to begin flight. For a brief moment, the weight transfers to the left picking foot.

Once the jump is at its full height, the feet are crossed, left over right, with toes pointed and legs pressed tightly together.

In single jumps the arms may be extended away from the body, but for multirotation jumps, the arms must pull in tightly against the body to speed up the spinning action.

- *Tapping the toe pick gently on takeoff.* The toe pick should not clobber the ice, causing spray and ice chunks.

History

- The toe loop is also called the cherry flip.
- American champion Tommy Litz was the first skater to land the triple toe loop, at the 1964 World Championships in Dortmund, Germany.
- Before his string of four World titles, Canadian Kurt Browning performed the first quadruple toe loop at the 1988 Worlds in Budapest.
- Another Canadian name hit the record books in 1991, when Elvis Stojko skated the first quad toe–double toe combination, and again at the 1994 Worlds, with the first quad toe–triple toe combination.
- The toe Wally was traditionally a separate jump from the toe loop, taking off from the same foot but from the opposite edge, a right back inside one. Now the distinction between the two jumps has become so minuscule that they are considered the same.

The Flip
(a toe jump)

1. Direction of takeoff? Backward (same as Salchow).
2. Type of edge? Inside (same as Salchow).
3. Is the toe pick used? Yes, this is a toe jump. (The only difference between the flip and the Salchow is that the latter is an edge jump.)

For the purposes of identification, think of the flip as a "toe Salchow."

Preparation and Takeoff

Despite the fact that the flip and the Salchow are closely related, the feeling of the flip is completely different. And there are some easy-to-spot differences.

First of all, think of both jumps as having two distinct shapes during their execution. Picture the skater with a felt-tipped pen attached to the bottom of her blade; the pen draws a black shadow on the ice throughout the jump. Here's what you'll see on the ice: The Salchow sketches a pronounced curve, usually skated across the ice, while the flip shows a much straighter line skated from end to end.

Another distinction lies in how the skater sets up the jump. If you remember, the Sal sits on the back inside edge on the takeoff, while the body readies itself for several seconds before jumping. In the flip, it's exactly the opposite. Before the skater even turns backward on the three, she sits posed on the forward edge, then makes a quick turn and an immediate pick with the right toe. When the pick is stabbed into the ice, the skater begins to transfer weight onto it. Unlike the Salchow, where the weight is on the left foot at the takeoff, in the flip, the takeoff is really from the toe of the right foot. And it's quick!

Bad

- *Curling the entry.* This makes the jump look too much like a Salchow and

FLIP OVERVIEW

Compare the flip with the Salchow. Both jumps begin from a left back inside edge (1), but in the flip, the right toe stabs the ice (2) to pull the feet and legs together (3) and to change the balance to the right foot (4) for the basic loop jump position (5–8).

FLIP DETAILS

Approaching the takeoff, but before the toe pick stabs the ice, the flip looks exactly like the Salchow. Both begin on a left back inside edge, with the right leg reaching behind and curving in a counterclockwise direction.

When the right toe picks the ice to vault the skater in the air, the action draws the feet and legs quickly together to begin the tightly tucked position of the basic loop jump.

When rotation is complete, the left leg moves away from the body by kicking forward. The right foot reaches for the ice, with the toe pick landing first and the weight gently moving farther backward along the blade.

changes the rhythm of the takeoff, reducing the jump to insignificance.

- *Poor takeoff position.* This causes the left toe to scratch, acting like a brake that slows the jump's speed so that it peters out by the time the skater lands.

Good

- *Strong right toe pick.* This sets the jump firmly into the air with the weight over the right foot.
- *Fast landing speed.* With the correct balance, the jump will appear to have as much speed on the landing as it did on the takeoff.

History

- A decade ago, as the simpler triples became commonplace, the highest achievement a skater could reach for was to succeed at the difficult triple Lutz. Somewhere in the confusion over triple development, the flip got overlooked and avoided. It was generally considered to belong to a class of triples that were much harder to perform than the toe or the Salchow, but not as difficult as the Lutz. Today, the jump is a must-have for top skaters, but one that must be carefully thought about and never taken for granted.

The Lutz
(a toe jump)

1. Direction of takeoff? Backward.
2. Type of edge? Outside.
3. Is the toe pick used? Yes, this is a toe jump.

Many skaters find the Lutz the most difficult jump because of its unique reverse entry. You just get going one way, then you have to turn around to jump in the opposite direction!

Preparation and Takeoff

This is a relatively easy jump to recognize. The characteristic long, diagonal entry makes spotting the Lutz simple but performing it hard.

The Lutz typically sits on the left back outside edge for what seems like forever while the skater glides toward the corner of the ice surface looking over his right shoulder. Some skaters vary this a little by gliding blind, not looking in the direction they're moving. If you were sitting up on the roof of the rink, the skater's pattern would look like a backward "S," making a wide curve on the ice in a clockwise direction as the skater approaches the jump.

The right foot reaches far behind to pick and the body seems naturally to want to start the rotation in the same clockwise manner. This is the tricky moment when the bottom curve of the backward "S" begins to take shape. The body must reverse its clockwise movement by turning in its normal direction but opposite to the takeoff. It's the entry that makes this jump so tough and explains why so many skaters have trouble with the takeoff.

Once the toe pick taps the ice, the legs are drawn tightly together, with the feet crossed and the arms close to the body as the whole torso stretches upward.

LUTZ OVERVIEW

The Lutz is recognizable by its long diagonal entry (2 and 3) and its S-shaped pattern when completed. The left back outside edge at the moment of the pick (4) means the skater must enter in a clockwise direction (1–4), then rotate counterclockwise (5–9) in the opposite direction. The Lutz is called a counterrotation jump, and the counterrotation significantly increases the difficulty.

 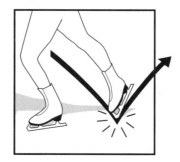 

LUTZ DETAILS

Sitting on the left back outside edge and curving clockwise, the skater waits for the perfect moment to swing the right foot behind to pick.

As the right toe picks into the ice in a line directly behind the left foot, the direction of rotation changes from clockwise at the entry to the jump to counterclockwise during the rotation and landing.

In the air the body is perfectly erect, with legs held tightly together and feet crossed left over right.

Bad

- *Changing the takeoff edge from outside to inside.* This is the single biggest problem for Lutz jumpers because it changes the basic character of the jump from a Lutz to a flip.
- *Landing on a back inside edge* instead of a back outside one. This indicates the skater has not successfully transferred his weight in the air to the landing foot.
- *Turning the shoulders before takeoff.* Skaters who do this ruin the timing of the body and begin the rotation before leaving the ice.

Good

- *Clearly defined back outside takeoff edge.* This emphasizes the Lutz technique.
- *Erect posture on takeoff.* Assuming this posture ensures that the body doesn't have to overwork by bending too far forward, which results in scratching and loss of speed.

History

- History is unclear about who invented the Lutz. I always thought it was a Mr. Lutz, but I can't find any source that confirms this.
- Canadian records show that Barbara Ann Scott was the first woman to perform the double Lutz, in a competition held in Winnipeg, Manitoba, in either 1947 or 1948.
- Prague, Czechoslovakia, became famous in skating circles in 1962 when Canadian Don Jackson landed the first triple Lutz and thus won the World Championship.
- In 1981, nearly twenty years later, Swiss World champion Denise Biellmann performed the first triple Lutz by a woman.
- In the years leading up to his Olympic gold medal in 1988, American Brian Boitano added an arm variation to the triple Lutz and made it his own. The "Tano" Lutz, with the left arm overhead during flight, is still as difficult and unusual today.

The Jump Combination

A jump combination is a succession of two or more jumps of at least one rotation in which the landing of the first jump is the takeoff for the second and so on. No turn or change of foot is allowed between the jumps, although the toe pick can be used to assist the takeoff of the second jump.

The combination differs from a jump sequence. In a sequence two or more jumps of any rotation are skated in rapid succession and turns or changes of feet are permitted. You will generally see more jumps in a sequence, but they will be jumps of lesser difficulty that require less speed to complete.

Preparation and Takeoff

At the elite level there have been exceptions, but the most common combination of all includes a second jump that is either the triple toe or the triple loop. Think about it. The landing of the first jump is always on the right back outside edge. Since there are no turns or changes of foot allowed, there are only two choices for the second jump, either the toe loop or the loop.

Bad

- *Poor first jump.* Such a jump sabotages the second one, which will fail due to poor balance or to poor timing and rhythm.
- *No speed on the landing of the first jump.* In this case the first jump dies, leaving no momentum to complete the second jump.
- *Changing feet, or turning before the next jump.* This may indicate bad technique on the first jump, or lack of concentration. The skater may be thinking only about the first jump, almost forgetting the second one.

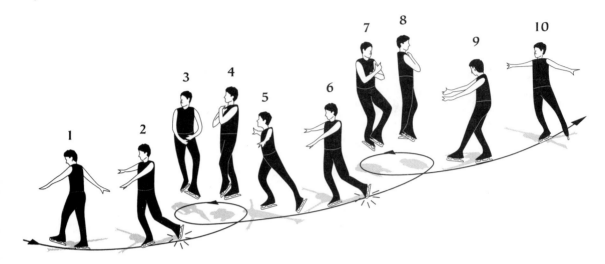

JUMP COMBINATION OVERVIEW

A legal jump combination is one where there are no turns or changes of feet between two separate jumps and where the landing of the first jump is the takeoff of the second. Here the landing of the first toe loop (5) is followed quickly (6) by the toe pick of a second toe loop takeoff, for a successful toe loop–toe loop combination.

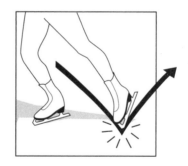

JUMP COMBINATION DETAIL

The first jump lands on the right back outside edge, and immediately the left toe pick stabs into the ice for the second toe loop takeoff.

Good

- *Fast and complete rotation.* The skater shows confidence, as if there were no landing between jumps.
- *Consistent speed through both jumps.* The second jump flows easily into the landing and doesn't peter out.

History

- The 1987 World champion, Brian Orser of Canada, was the first skater to complete a triple–triple combination.
- Midori Ito from Japan was the first woman to perform a triple combination, a triple loop–triple loop, at the 1981 World Junior Championships.
- Canadian champion Brian Pockar chose a very unusual combination, a one-foot double Axel–triple Salchow. He used the left forward outside edge on the Axel takeoff, landing on the same foot but on the left back inside edge, a risky setup for the takeoff of the Sal. It required a perfect double Axel; without one, the Sal could be kissed goodbye.
- A quad toe–double toe hit the skating world in 1991, when Elvis Stojko competed at the Worlds. And it was at the 1994 Worlds in Chiba, Japan, that Elvis once again made news by successfully landing the first quad toe–triple toe.
- As of the 1997 skating season, the most difficult combinations include the triple Axel with another triple jump, either the toe or the loop, and the quad toe combined with the triple toe.

The Spins: Getting the Facts

Spins are by far the most underrated element in figure skating. Although the skating world is beginning to pay attention to them, good spinners are not rewarded for their skills the way jumpers are compensated for theirs.

Don't get me wrong. A good jump is hard to do, and if you're a fan who wants to find out just how hard, try a jump on your living-room floor or in your backyard. You may not be able to do a triple Axel just yet, but you can get the breathtaking feeling of a jump, even away from the ice.

Spinning is completely different. Oh, sure, jumping and spinning rely on some of the same tricks, but it's only when a person gets into a pair of skates and onto a rink that it becomes possible to defy gravity for more than a split second. Nowhere else in the world, except maybe hanging from a trapeze, can you experience what it's like to spin! Ballet and modern dancers can get close, but floor resistance makes it impossible to approach the potential offered on ice. When a spin is properly done on ice, it wins the war against friction.

Here's how. A spin happens when the skater has learned to overcome and control two major forces over an extended time. These forces are: centripetal, the force from the skater as she pulls her arms and legs tightly toward the center axis of her body; and centrifugal, the force from the spin that pushes the arms and legs of the skater away from her body. The balance of these two forces produces a dazzling effect. And, no, skaters don't get dizzy!

Ballet dancers "spot" their rotation to avoid getting dizzy by moving their head at a different rate from the rest of the body and by focusing on some point on the horizon. Well, in skating, everyone starts out being dizzy when they're learning the basics, but as the individual's control and skill progresses, dizziness disappears. He rarely gets lost. The skater develops an extra sense—the ability to see the world as it whizzes by, without really looking at it. It's funny, but competitive skaters can even tell in a fast spin which way they must face when they finish.

During my own competitive years, I was once in a bad accident in which I fell from the top of a lift. There was no blood, thank goodness, but I was unconscious. The doctors had difficulty figuring out whether I was seriously injured, and although they eventually diagnosed a skull fracture, no amount of testing by holding me upside down could make me dizzy. I guess you could call this one of the perks of being a competitive pair skater!

What to look for

Top-notch spins will be centered, fast, beautiful, creative and long-lasting.

The first thing to look for in a spin is whether it takes place in one spot. Skaters call this being *centered*. On the ice the skate will draw tiny, repetitive circles, about four to five inches in diameter, that constantly trace over each other. If the circles begin to wander across the ice, even for a short distance, the spin is said to be "traveling," which is a no-no. Staying centered is possible only if the body is standing perfectly erect. Imagine how a puppet dangles from its strings, or how it would feel to stretch your body to make it taller.

As with any element in skating, *speed* is a definite plus, but we're not talking about ice coverage here. In a spin, speed refers to how quickly the rotations occur. A slow spin, that is one that doesn't rotate quickly, is easier to center because the forces being exerted on the skater are not as strong. Whenever speed is increased, the force also increases and all the other qualities of a good spin become harder to achieve. Like a good jump, a spin should maintain its speed. A spin that begins fast, then loses speed quickly until it peters out, is clearly not as desirable as one that "blurs" right to the end.

When a spin is done in a beautiful *position*, you have the feeling you'd like to watch it forever. Because there are only four basic spinning positions, judges will give considerable weight to *creativity* when assigning marks. The forces change anytime a spin alters position, so the real challenge is to be innovative and complicated without interrupting the spin's speed and center.

Rules have become very strict in order to encourage spins of long *duration*. Watch great spinners such as American Scott Davis or Lucinda Ruh from Switzerland. Their spinning technique is so awesome and their speed so exceptional that their blades don't even seem to touch the ice. They float! Another Swiss skater, Nathalie Krieg, is in the *Guinness Book of Records* for performing the longest spin in history—a combination spin that went on for more than three minutes.

Senior competitors must spin for a minimum of eight revolutions in the required position for spins in the short program, not including the flying spin (six revolutions) or the combination spin (twelve revolutions).

The stages of a spin

There are four important stages in the execution of any spin: *preparation*, the way the skater sets the spin up on the ice; *entry*, how the spin begins; *position*, what form or posture is required; and *exit*, how the skater leaves. But what gives a spin its individuality is the second and third stages, the entry and the position.

Unlike jumps, whose preparations are all unique, certain stages in spins are identical when first learned. Restricted only by their ability and imagination, more advanced competitors will use a preparation or an exit that is unusual or sudden, making the success of the spin an even greater achievement, but for our purposes we will stick to something more ordinary.

For the sake of simplicity, we'll study six basic spins that all have two stages in common: the preparation and the exit.

Preparation

The most common method of preparing for a spin is from backward crosscuts skated in the opposite direction to the rotation of the spin. If the spin turns counterclockwise, the backward crosscuts are skated in a clockwise direction. The skater provides a clue that a spin is on the way when she winds up her shoulders by bringing her right arm back while keeping her left arm in front and holding a strong right back inside edge with the left free foot extended behind. The skater then steps forward to start the entry to the spin and turns a left forward outside three to begin spinning.

Exit

By releasing the tight positions of the arms and legs and opening up the body, the skater can push away from the center of the spin onto a right back outside edge.

Identifying spins

There are zillions of possible positions, but once the skater is spinning like a top, there are only four main groups of spinning positions: the *upright*, the *camel*, the *sit* and the *layback*. Again assuming the skater is spinning in a counterclockwise direction, these four can be broken down further into either forward, done on the left foot, or backward, done on the right.

I need to make an important distinction here. When referring to spins, the terms forward and backward indicate what foot the skater is on. To repeat, forward is on the left, backward is on the right. It has absolutely nothing to do with whether you're on a forward or backward edge during the actual spin. In fact, with the exception of some original variations, the goal of all spins is to reduce friction by turning on the flat of the blade or, in other words, on both edges at the same time. The reality, though, is a little different. Skaters attempt to spin as close to a flat as possible but generally compromise by spinning in small back circles. For a forward spin, they do this on a slight back inside edge on the left foot; for a backward spin, on a slight back outside edge on the right foot.

Before we get into the specific spins and their unique characteristics, let's add a few more spin words to your vocabulary: The terms *change*, *flying* and *combination* identify variations that increase the difficulty of the spin.

- *Change* refers to a change of foot.
- A *flying spin* is one that is entered from a jump and that is landed in the spinning position, as in flying camel or flying sit. The skater must hold the required position for at least eight revolutions.
- A *spin combination* is a spin incorporating a change of foot and a minimum of at least three basic positions, such as sit, camel and upright. Judges will be counting the turns. In the senior short, at least six rotations must be done on each foot, for a minimum total of twelve, not including the wind-up.

Train your eye to figure out which foot the skater is on—left for forward and right for backward—combine that information with the spinning position—upright, camel, sit or layback—notice if the spin is spiced with a few variations, and you will be able to identify the spin.

The Corkscrew Spin (forward upright)

The corkscrew is one of several upright spins based on the simple one-foot spin; the "barber pole" effect it creates makes it easy to recognize. After a skater first experiments with controlling the body during prolonged rotation on the basic one-foot spin, he advances to the more challenging corkscrew.

If you listen to the sound created by a few spins, you will discover that most of them are relatively quiet because they are done behind the toe pick. In the corkscrew, however, the skater is balanced farther forward, close to the front of the foot at the point on the blade where the bottom toe pick begins to scrape the ice, giving the spin a distinctive, scratchy sound. This is one reason why it's so important when you buy your first pair of skates not to shave off the toe picks, no matter what some hockey hack says. You need them, just like you need your toes, for balance. The picks may get in the way when you're first learning how to glide and stroke, but I promise, you'll adjust quickly. Trust me on this one.

Entry

After the wind-up is complete, the skater pushes forward with a softly bent knee onto a deeply curved left forward outside three-turn, bringing the shoulders and arms forcefully around to a natural position to begin the rotation. At the same time, the right leg begins to swing around the body to the front.

Position

Speed will increase dramatically as the hands clasp together in front of the body and as the right foot begins to make its way to a position resting slightly above the skating knee. The skating knee now begins to straighten. And the spin is still getting faster. At this stage, the force trying to pull the arms and legs away from the body is immense,

CORKSCREW SPIN DETAIL

Following the entry, the upper body returns to a neutral position, facing forward with arms held evenly on each side.

The right leg moves in a circular path around the body from behind to in front. The spinning foot traces tiny left back inside circles centered on one spot on the ice.

The speed of the spin increases as the hands clasp in front and the right foot crosses over the left knee. The spin remains centered.

At its fastest point, the spin is a blur. The arms are stretched down the torso and held tightly against the body. The right foot is now crossed securely over the left, with the legs pressed firmly together.

and it takes every ounce of strength the skater has to remain in control. The arms pull into the body at the same time as the right foot slides down the skating leg until the ankles are crossed. The spin is now nothing but a blur!

Bad

- *Losing the center* by letting the body sway back and forth or by rocking on the blade and constantly changing the point of balance and therefore changing the center.
- *Failing to hit the correct position.* This happens when the force is so great that the arms and legs cannot sustain their tight placement against the body.

Good

- *Speed increases easily.* The skater appears to be in control and does not struggle to hold form.
- *Spin is long-lasting.* There is not just one burst of speed, but a continuous velocity over an extended period of time.

History

- The corkscrew is also called the scratch spin, for obvious reasons.
- It is usually skated as the concluding spin position in all other spins.
- It may also be skated backward, i.e., on the right foot.
- American Ronnie Robertson, 1956 Olympic and World silver medalist, won the free skating portions of the events with a spinning technique that earned him the moniker "The Human Blur." He was eventually clocked in his corkscrew spin at nearly 160 kph (100 mph)!

The Camel Spin (forward camel)

The camel spin is an easy one to spot. With the body horizontal to the ice and the free leg lifted behind, the camel looks like a spiral in a spin. It's a beautiful position when done well, but it's never a position in which the skater can relax. Because the body is constantly stretching to maintain the spiral, it's considered one of the most strenuous spins in the business.

Entry

The camel has several quirky elements. Unlike any upright spin that uses the action of the right leg swinging in front to start the rotation, the horizontal position of the body in the camel requires the right leg to stay behind during the entry. Then, at the perfect moment, as the upper body flattens and bends parallel to the ice, the right leg and foot are quickly raised to be at least even in height with the head.

You will often see skaters hit the toe pick at this point and spin very far forward on the blade for the first rotation. This sets everything in motion, allowing the body to spin around the skating foot.

Position

Variations in arm positions give the camel many different looks, but the overriding picture is one of extension and elegance. The right leg drops at the end of the spin and swings in front to wind up the spin in an upright or corkscrew position.

Bad

- *Bad position.* Bent legs with poor turn-out, a hunched back or sloppy arm placement reduce the beauty of the spin.
- *Spinning too far up on the toe pick.* This reduces the speed of the rotation and threatens the balance of the skater.

CAMEL SPIN DETAIL

The final moments of the preparation have the skater "wind up" on the right back inside edge, ready to step forward on the left outside edge to begin the spin entry. Notice how the left arm has moved in front and the right arm has moved behind to complete the "wind-up."

With a strong forward push onto the left outside edge, the right foot and blade power up to give the spin its initial speed. The whole body begins to turn to the left.

Unlike most other spins, the right free leg does not swing around during the entry to the camel spin but stays behind the body, ready to move into the spiral position. The left knee is deeply bent for control and the upper body anticipates bending toward the ice.

When the left foot three-turns backward, the upper body bends forward, bellybutton facing the ice surface, and the right leg lifts into a spiral, creating a body line that is parallel to the ice. The whole body must stretch to the max.

Good

- *Fast rotation.* With the body so spread out, superb stretch and control are required for fast rotation.
- *Extra arm and body movement that maintain the basic nature of the spin.* Any additional movement adds value as long as the spin maintains its center.

History

- In the past, a camel spin was considered to be a feminine spin, so it was uncommon to see a man in a very extended position. If you did, their heads were always higher than their feet and the spiral looked horrible.
- Camel spins have become so important that new versions have been invented. In the best one the skater actually flips from a backward inside edge to a forward outside edge. Back in the seventies, Toller Cranston of Canada was the first male skater to elevate the camel spin to an art form.

The Flying Camel Spin (backward camel)

Here comes one of those special *spin* words. A flying camel spin is just a camel that begins with a unique kind of jump. A legal description of a flying spin is one that hits its chosen position in the air and continues in that position after the landing, with one little additional challenge. Before the skater jumps, she is not permitted to have performed any previous rotation on the ice.

Entry

As the skater pushes onto the left forward outside edge, she appears to launch her body into the air, not in the normal vertical way for a regular jump, but in a more horizontal manner as if she were doing a cartwheel without touching the ice with her hands. The legs swing out and behind the skater, with the left leg kicking higher than the right. As the right foot reaches down to the ice to land, the left leg has already hit the camel position. Approximately one full rotation has been turned, but it will look like the skater has taken off and landed in the same spot on the ice.

The jump covers no distance and, in fact, on a good flying camel jump, the skater will have found her center the instant she lands.

Position

Changing feet from takeoff to landing has turned this camel spin from forward to backward, or from left foot to right. The flying camel has an easier feel to the rotation than its forward cousin because of the natural turning-out of the body in this direction.

Position variations may include such things as spinning on a bent knee, turning the shoulders and head to look up rather than down, or changing arm placement to emphasize accents in the music.

FLYING CAMEL SPIN DETAIL

On the forward entry, as the right leg swings around the skater jumps into the air.

During the jump the body is horizontal, like a cartwheel but without the hands touching the ice. The jump should take off and land in approximately the same place and not travel any distance across the ice.

While the skater is changing feet to land, the left leg must already be in camel position, with the body stretched out parallel to the ice.

Balanced now on the right foot, the skater traces tiny backward outside circles.

Bad

- *Jumping across the ice.* Going for ice coverage in the jump will make the spin travel and lose its center.
- *Jumping with the body in a vertical position to the ice.* This eliminates the possibility of attaining the camel position during the jump. The body remains upright in the air instead of being parallel to the ice.
- *Letting the ankle fall over on takeoff or landing.* If this happens, the jump will be puny and the landing may wander for several spins, losing speed.

Good

- *Big jump with definite camel position in the air.* This shows confidence and control.
- *Spin hits its center immediately on landing.* The resulting fast rotation indicates strong form and technique; the left leg has been aggressive in getting to the spiral position.

History

- American Olympic and World champion Dick Button was the first skater to popularize the flying camel, although he did not invent this spin. To many skaters it is still called the Button camel.
- In the early 1970s, Canadian Toller Cranston again perfected another element in the flying camel preparation by ignoring all the tried and true methods and developing a unique entry, which consisted of a series of very fast forward outside–backward inside three-turns eventually leading to the takeoff of the spin.
- Other American variations came from 1976 Olympic champion Dorothy Hamill, who created the Hamill camel. This spin is similar to a flying camel except that it involves a quick change to a backward sit spin after a short rotation in the back camel position.
- The flying camel changes feet from takeoff to landing, but this isn't necessarily the case in all flying spins. For instance, in the true flying sit spin, the skater takes off and lands on the same foot.

The Sit Spin
(forward or backward)

The compulsory position in this spin is what a beginner learns as a "shoot-the-duck." This involves crouching down and gliding on one foot in a straight line with the other foot out in front, "taking aim." (I always thought this was much harder to do gliding than spinning.)

Entry

As with the upright spin, the skater steps forward to enter and brings the right leg around to begin rotation, but now with more force and in a wider circle than in the corkscrew. At the same time, the skater bends the skating knee so the body moves down into a sitting position until the upper part of the leg is parallel to the ice.

Position

There are several different schools of thought about what constitutes the best position for the sit spin. Depending on personal style and body build, the skater may bend so far down to the ice that he seems to have his rear end resting on the heel of his spinning foot while he holds his shoot-the-duck foot out perfectly straight. Male skaters seem to favor this style.

Women, on the other hand, tend to prefer a spin that is not as low to the ice, where the right leg is slightly bent around the skating leg, with the foot held closer to the ice and the body leaning forward at about a thirty-degree angle from the upright position.

When skaters are learning the sit, they often try to help themselves balance by leaning on their spinning knee. Not only does this look unattractive, but it gets in the way, making it impossible to bend the body far enough forward to hold the sitting position comfortably. And if they try to press their knees together during the spin, it becomes difficult to stand up again without putting the other foot down for more support.

SIT SPIN DETAIL

As the right leg swings around, the left knee bends very deeply and the body leans forward from the hips to balance over the left knee.

Once the right leg pulls completely in front, the body will be moving to a full sitting position.

Arm and leg styles may vary, as long as the spin is fast, centered and beautiful.

A better pose is to have the arms stretched downward and in front along a similar path to the shoot-the-duck leg.

Exit

Once the sit is finished, the skater merely stands up on one foot and completes the spin in the usual way.

Bad

- *Starting the spin in an upright position.* This adds a stage of extra motion that the skater may find difficult to control.
- *Failing to bring the right leg around in a wide enough circle.* This reduces the potential for speed and may create a rocking movement on the blade.

Good

- *Spin has consistent speed.* This shows off the skater's good balance and indicates that he is spinning on the right part of the blade.
- *Sit position seems comfortable and restful.* If the skater appears to be relaxed, the audience will also feel this way.

History

- Some related spins include the flying sit, a spin commenced with a jump in the sit position; but unlike the flying camel, which changes feet to land, the take-off and landing of the flying sit are on the same foot.
- The broken leg is a sit spin with an attitude. Instead of the free foot extending out in front, the right leg "breaks" at the knee and hangs off to the right side just above the ice. These spins are very rare today because they are generally much slower in rotation and can look very awkward if the position is incorrect.
- You might lose a few teeth when learning the death drop. However, its name is much scarier than the actual spin. To give you an idea of what to look for when assessing spins, the death drop is a cross between a flying camel and a back sit, taking off with greater speed and more ice coverage; it's like a huge flying camel. After the landing, the skater will hit the back camel position for a microsecond and then flip over to a back sit spin.

The Layback Spin (forward or backward)

This spin can be recognized by the skater's deeply arched upper body as she bends at the hips to lean straight back over the skating foot. The sideways leaning spin, or the side-back, is a different form of this spin. Here the skater leans to the side instead of straight back. Usually, if the skater has an excellent spiral, her flexibility will also result in a superbly skated layback.

Remember, to avoid mark deductions, senior skaters need to spin for *at least* eight revolutions in this spin.

Entry

As the skater pushes onto the left forward outside edge, the spin looks almost identical to the corkscrew, but as the moment comes to move the right foot across to rest on the front of the left knee, exactly the reverse happens. The lower part of the right leg, from the knee down to the foot, either moves behind into an attitude position, slightly bent with the knee turned open as in the standard layback, or it drops to the side of the left foot and slightly behind with the knee straight as in the side-back.

At the same time as the right leg moves behind, the upper body bends from the hips and drops backward all in one movement, stretching the head upside down, and elongating the front of the chest and stomach. It's as if the skater is trying to get a bird's-eye view of the ceiling.

Position

The more the skater arches her back, the more her hips push out in front to balance. If you could freeze the action at this moment on the skater's full body profile, the position of the head and back, the free leg and free foot would form the shape of a "C."

LAYBACK SPIN DETAIL

The layback entry is similar to the corkscrew spin entry, with the right leg swinging in a circle around the body until the spin is centered.

Speed increases as the body arches backward from the hips. At the same time, the right leg bends and moves behind the body in an attitude position to counterbalance the forward movement of the hips. Variations on arm and free-leg positions are allowed.

The skater can enhance this exquisite picture by moving her arms and hands in time with the music. But those movements can also increase the speed and difficulty of the spin. As is the case with the Biellmann, at first glance you'd never believe anything could happen in this position, but the arrangement of the body around its axis capitalizes on the forces at work to create a thing of beauty.

Exit

Before exiting the spin in the normal manner, the skater must get back into the upright position by rolling the body up to vertical one vertebrae at a time, beginning with the lower back and leaving the head till last.

Bad

- *Leaning back with only the shoulders and head instead of from the hips.* If this happens, the position is only partly completed. Moreover, this causes the spin to either balance too far forward on the toe or too far backward on the heel.
- *Dropping the spinning ankle over to the inside of the foot.* This results in traveling and disorientation. In this laid-back position, the skater feels more vulnerable to problems.

Good

- *Bending back quickly.* The skater finds the center soon after entry and assumes the position immediately to take advantage of the initial speed.
- *Lifting right free leg fairly high off the ice during the spin.* This demonstrates further flexibility in the hips.

History

- The layback has unlimited use in the free program, but in the short program, it's an isolated element only for women, although men have been known to use it creatively in the spin combination.
- Often the side-back and the layback will be combined to become one giant layback accentuating the flexibility of the skater and her ability to lean in all directions.

The Biellmann Spin (forward or backward)

Typically, the Biellmann spin originates with a camel or layback spin in which the skater grabs the blade of her free foot, changes position and pulls her foot and leg high above her head while still holding on with both hands.

Very few spinners have been able to perform the spin well enough to include it as an isolated element. Usually women perform it as a concluding position in a long combination spin, and even then, the number of those is small.

Entry

The camel spin is a great warm-up for the Biellmann. Once the camel is under way, the skater raises her upper body to the vertical position, lowering the spiraling leg and reaching behind to find the blade.

The layback provides another potential way of moving into the Biellmann. The free leg is handy and the right hand is close by, ready to find the foot.

Instead of grabbing the bottom of the blade, which is sharp, the skater usually grabs the steel post that connects the blade to the heel support attached to the boot. If she's doing a forward Biellmann, the fingers of her right hand make the connection with the right blade, and if she does a backward Biellmann, she uses her left hand to grab the steel post on her left foot.

Position

Once the hold is solid, the spin begins to look like a pretzel, with the skater pulling the spiraling leg up from behind and then over her head. Flexibility is the key to this spin. Not only must the angle between the spiraling leg and the spinning leg form an almost perfect 180 degrees, but the skater's upper body and back need to be made out of nothing more rigid than cartilage. This kind of elasticity can only be found in skaters who are quadruple-jointed. (Of course, they don't exist, but you know what I mean!)

BIELLMANN SPIN DETAIL

The layback is the perfect setup for the Biellmann spin.

During the backward arch of the layback, the skater balances and prepares to grab the blade of the right foot with the right hand.

As the skater pulls her right foot over her head with her right hand, her left hand also reaches for the blade and pulls it overhead to add strength to the movement. The legs form a completely vertical split position.

The body, arms and legs are pulled more closely to the center axis of the spin as it extends beyond the skater's head, and the spin accelerates at great speed. *Really* good ones can exceed twenty rotations!

But, listen, this is no run-of-the-mill spin. I can't imagine being able to get into the position in the first place, but then to have to spin too. . . .

Bad

- *Sloppy and awkward form while reaching for the free foot.* Fumbling for the foot slows down the spin and uses up precious momentum. When the Biellmann position is finally achieved, the resulting spin is too slow and too short.
- *Unable to hold the required position for more than one or two rotations.* The spin never really succeeds except as a fleeting pose.

Good

- *Transition to Biellmann is fast and sure.* This enables the spin to remain centered.
- *Spin accelerates.* This gives the spin a long duration and shows body control and flexibility.

History

- Denise Biellmann of Switzerland invented the Biellmann spin on her way to winning the World Championship in 1981. Many skaters have attempted this spin, but it's interesting to note that the majority who have succeeded have also been Swiss.
- Nathalie Krieg, a Swiss competitor who competed in the 1994 Olympic Games, maintained that because she trained on such a small-sized ice surface, the only things she could consistently practice were her spins. The result? Another incredible Biellmann.
- Lucinda Ruh, also an international competitor from Switzerland, gave her father the Biellmann spin for his birthday. She'd been practicing it in secret!

Pair Skating: Getting the Facts

What is pair skating and how does it differ from dance? Both disciplines stress the importance of unison when two people are skating together. In pairs, the unison must be performed while free skating to music and doing difficult jumps, spins and lifts, but in dance, although simple jumps, spins and lifts may be used, the emphasis is on performing creative dance steps and other movements that express the character of the music.

If I may be so vulgar, think circus when you watch pairs, and think ballroom when you watch dance.

An excellent pair-skating team is made up of two individuals who are outstanding free skaters in their own right, and who simultaneously skate moves either symmetrically, like mirror images, or parallel, like shadows.

Body types may be strikingly similar or drastically different, but according to the rules, whatever the shapes and sizes of the respective partners, their movements together should create the overall impression of "a single composition." The partners may not always be performing exactly the same steps, and they may even separate from time to time, but watching good pair skating will give you the impression of harmony; both skaters understand the same on-ice patterns and have identical program goals.

As a pair skater, you're never alone. Reaching out for the hand of your partner is like finding your root. The team should work like a well-oiled machine, creating a unique entity worth more than the sum of the individuals' skills.

It's not a sport for the faint of heart. If a skater gets airsick with both feet off the ice at the same time, she should choose something different. This kind of skating demands massive amounts of courage: Both partners need to have absolute trust in each other and share mutual respect. Think about it. When you're cruising across the rink at 30 kph (18.6 mph), launching into a lift, you need to know your partner is doing everything in his power to keep you safe. And it's not just the women who are in danger. Men get beaten up, too, by wayward elbows, knees in the wrong places, and feet with sharp things on the bottom.

It's the danger factor. Sometimes, even with the best of intentions, people collide and accidents happen. Of course, when speed and height are increased as in pair skating, the potential for error also increases. The ice is *hard* and quite unforgiving, and it chooses the most inappropriate moments to point out mistakes. In fact, during the learning stages of elements, most pair skaters suffer from terrible falls and repeated injuries that no amount of crash-padding can eliminate. And every pair team knows that even when you're at the top of the game, you can count on a couple of killer accidents every season.

So why do it? Why take the risks? Why entrust your health and well-being to someone else on the basis of a promise? Because it's as close to flying as you're ever going to get!

What to look for

Now that you're an expert at identifying the jumping and spinning elements from singles skating, let's move on and add the most common pair elements to that ever-expanding list, remembering that pair skating also includes individual jumps and spins.

Good pair skating has all the same goals as other skating disciplines: speed, flow, form, control, deep edges, power, strength and endurance. The added pair elements, like lifts, throws, pair spins and death spirals, demand even more of skaters because they require different skills from single skating and present a whole new battery of possibilities for content.

Lifts are assisted jumps that break down into three basic categories: *overheads*, *hip lifts* and *twists*. Each one must be skated with a continual ascending and descending rotational movement, with the man's arms fully extended at the top of the lift. The ascending and descending action may be interrupted for a maximum of three revolutions. On the big lifts, no carrying of the partner is permitted on either the man's back, shoulders or knees, although as long as his hands don't reach above his shoulders, the man may assist in small lifts that include any type of hold up to a duration of one and a half rotations.

Quality lifts are like quality jumps—high, fast and powerful. The partners should display beautiful form and style no matter how difficult the components of the lift may be. The woman should always appear confident, and for most lifts her body posture and leg extension need to be extremely strong, not only for aesthetic reasons, but for safety concerns as well. Any hesitation or doubt on her part, reflected in sagging or weak positions, can cause the man either to lose his balance or to lose control, spelling disaster for the lift.

The man's role as the support in the lift requires him to be perfectly balanced at all times, turning cleanly and easily from one foot to the other during rotation so as to maintain speed and ice coverage. Any lift that is well done will show a seamless series of movements and position changes in which the respective partners seem to be attached by an invisible thread from takeoff to landing.

Throws need to be in their own category despite the fact that the woman is assisted on the takeoff, just as in a lift. That's where the similarity ends. Once the woman is airborne in a throw, she becomes a totally free projectile and must perform most of the move on her own, landing without any support from her partner.

Pair spins are based on positions from singles skating: upright, camel, sit and layback. What makes them so much fun are the possible variations, things that work as a pair that would never work performed alone. Pair or solo, however, the same standards apply: definite centers, fast rotation, creative and beautiful positions, and long duration.

It's a dynamite name, but frankly, the term *death spiral* is a misnomer. In all my years in the sport, I have never heard of anyone getting injured doing one. The best death spirals are long and fast, the man in pivot position for at least one full rotation, the woman arched backward with the top of her head almost touching the ice.

Identifying lifts in pair skating

Lifts are the most difficult elements to define because often one lift may incorporate form and technique from as many as three or four different lifts. The descriptions that follow will give you the basics, but please keep in mind that pair skaters are wildly inventive.

Once again, the first thing to watch is the *woman's* takeoff, and then answer the three questions that apply to jumping: Is she skating forward or backward? Is she on an inside or an outside edge? And does she use her toe pick on the takeoff? Since all the lift entrances are based on those of the solo jumps, answering these questions will certainly give you a good head start.

The next thing to watch is how the partners are holding each other. Are they holding hands, or are the man's hands on the woman's hips, or is it some combination of both?

A few years ago, pair elements were considered to be fairly boring and predictable. However, things have changed. With the encouragement of and rewards for innovation and creativity, and with the improvement in the caliber of individual skating today, the technical and artistic possibilities for pairs have become limitless.

As you begin to study the individual pair moves and how to recognize them, remember that this selection is only composed of the six most common pair elements—three types of lifts, throws, pair spins and death spirals.

The Overhead Lift

The term overhead describes a variety of lifts with one thing in common, the woman's position at the top of the lift. Names and takeoffs may vary from a lasso to a platter to a toe overhead, but in all these similar lifts, once the woman is in flight, she is balanced vertically over the man's shoulders with her back arched and her legs generally in split position.

The lasso, the original overhead lift from which all these new generation lifts are derived, is considered to be the most difficult of the overhead lifts for the same reason that the Axel is the most difficult solo jump—because of the forward takeoff.

Preparation

Crank up that speed!

Most lifts are placed diagonally on the ice. The skaters move into the takeoff from backward crosscuts to maximize speed and ice coverage, holding hands while they do so. In the lasso the skaters usually move closer together as they near the takeoff, left hand to left hand and right to right. It's interesting to note here that every team has its own quirky way of holding hands, depending on the nature of the lift. My partner and I never held hands in an ordinary way. We found that our strength and balance were better if my hand encircled his thumb rather than the more usual method of grasping palms.

With a special grip, there is less chance of slipping. That's why you'll notice pair skaters never wear gloves, even on the coldest days in the coldest rinks!

Takeoff

The forward entry and the swinging nature of the woman's takeoff really test the partner's control and technique. Since the toe pick cannot be used in the lasso, the stability

PAIR OVERHEAD LIFT OVERVIEW

As the pair approach the lift with backward crosscuts (1), the handhold changes and the woman steps forward (2) to take off in an Axel style by kicking the right foot forward, aiming up the man's left side and around his back (3). Using his left hand as the pivot point (3), the man lifts the woman up to full extension (4 and 5) in a split position. In the dismount, the reverse occurs, with the woman's weight now over the man's right hand (6) as he gently lowers her to the ice for the landing (7).

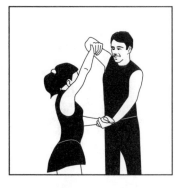

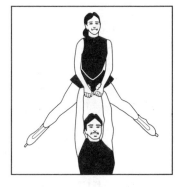

PAIR OVERHEAD LIFT DETAIL

Prior to lifting, the hands hold right to right and left to left, with the left hands lower to serve as the pressure point to begin the ascending motion.

The woman's circular path around and behind the man begins as the right leg kicks up his left side and around his back. Timing is critical. The woman jumps first and the man capitalizes on that action by lifting at the moment of the woman's weightlessness.

This is the perfect overhead position. Both partners' arms are fully extended, with the woman beautifully poised over the man's head, back arched, legs split and toes pointed.

and timing of the lifting movement is crucial for both skaters. It means the difference between a lift that sails easily to its summit and one that looks like a weight-lifting contest.

During the takeoff, the woman must bend the right free leg and kick it up in the direction of her left shoulder, springing off her left foot as she feels the effects of her kick. As she begins her takeoff, the man bends even lower to get under her jump and, at the moment of her weightlessness, presses the lift up even higher until both partners' arms are fully extended.

Spectators may think that pair skaters have to be body-builders. There's no question that strength is important—skaters need it to be able to sustain and control their movements—but you don't have to be Arnold Schwarzenegger to become a good pair skater. It's all timing, knowing the right moment to jump and the right moment to lift.

Flight

Once the lasso reaches its highest point, the woman will be in the characteristic pose with back arched, head erect and legs stretched in a split position with toes pointed. At this moment, when the woman's rotation has paused, the man may begin to rotate, and/or the woman may change position. It is important to note that every alteration in the plain path of the lift adds to the degree of difficulty.

Here's a question. While a pair is skating, who do you watch, the man or the woman? Most people watch the woman. She's supposed to be center stage. Next time, try watching the man and, in particular, look at his feet during the lifts. If he's doing his job well, you'll see him gliding easily; you won't see any snow or hear any scraping sounds as he turns from one foot to the other.

Landing

Lifts will land when the man gently lowers the woman onto a right back outside edge. Since unison is so important in pairs, as the man settles the woman back to the ice, he will also assume a forward position that mirrors hers.

Bad

- *Failure to reach full arms' height.* Poor timing between partners prevents the lift from reaching its peak. It may cause the woman to slide down the man's back, or may force the pair to simplify the lift's difficulty.

- *Scraping and scratching of man's feet during rotation.* This slows the lift's speed and jars the balance of both partners.
- *Woman falls out of lift onto a heavy landing.* When this happens, the man has not supported the landing sufficiently, or instead of keeping pressure in her body, the woman has collapsed during the exit.

Good

- *Woman hits required position quickly.* This shows teamwork and good timing on the takeoff.
- *High speed is maintained, with good ice coverage.* This demonstrates proper balance.
- *Complicated position changes increase the difficulty.* If the changes are smoothly done without interrupting the flow, they enhance the quality of the lift.

History

- Canadians Frances Dafoe and Norris Bowden were World pair champions in 1954 and 1955, but lost the 1956 Olympic gold medal in one of the sport's most controversial decisions. The team had added to its performance never-before-seen overhead lifts and throws, elements not covered in the rules. Without appropriate guidelines, the judges were lost and Dafoe and Bowden suffered the consequences by finishing second.
- By 1959, rules regarding the number of rotations in a lift were changed to permit two (and later three) revolutions, as long as the arms were fully extended.

The Split Lutz Twist (lift)

This twist is a combination of a throw and a lift, entered backward from a Lutz preparation. The difference between a twist and a throw is primarily in the landing: for the twist, the man catches the woman at the waist before she lands, whereas in a throw, it's "Bye, bye, Mr. Spalding!" as the woman fights to land the jump without any help from her partner.

Preparation

As you might expect from the name, the Lutz twist is set up like the Lutz jump, on a backward diagonal across the rink using backward crosscuts. With the man leading, the couple pulls closely together as the man holds the woman at her waist, her hands pressing firmly down on his wrists. In preparation for takeoff, the woman reaches behind to pick with her toe.

Takeoff

Both partners bend deeply to initiate the jump, the man on two feet and the woman on her left with the right toe pick placed in behind. The woman stabs her pick in one of two places, either to the man's extreme left at the outside of his body, or in between his feet, according to the skaters' choice. Both techniques are effective.

Flight

On the way up, the actual flight begins not with a twist or a spin, but with a quick split by the woman as she senses the need to wind up for the real rotation. As she approaches the top of the lift, she pulls her legs back together with her feet crossed, at the exact moment her partner spins her free of his hold.

The key to this lift is to get the spin up high enough in the air that the woman can complete the revolutions with time to spare before being caught and returned to the ice.

PAIR SPLIT LUTZ TWIST OVERVIEW

Preparing from clockwise back crosscuts (1), the man places his hands on the woman's hips (2) as she reaches behind to pick with her right foot (3). The man assists as the woman jumps. On the way to the top of the lift (4), the woman splits and is then tossed in the air (5) as she pulls her legs together and rotates free of the man's hold. When the rotation is complete, and before the woman touches the ice, the man catches her (6) and settles her gently back on to the ice (7).

PAIR SPLIT LUTZ TWIST DETAIL

Like the solo Lutz jump, the woman travels on a left back outside edge as she reaches in behind to pick with the right foot.

In the hold, the man's hands are placed securely on the woman's hips. While he lifts, she presses down forcefully on his wrists to stop them from sliding up her body and reducing the height of the lift.

On the landing, the man catches the woman at the waist after she finishes rotating but before she hits the ice.

Landing

When the woman's spin is finished, whether it's one, two or three revolutions, the man catches her at the waist and places her smoothly onto one foot on the right back outside edge.

Bad

- *Starting the spin too soon.* When this happens, the lift fails to reach its full height, which creates a situation where there's too little time to complete the spin before landing.
- *Incomplete rotation.* The woman is still spinning as she lands, forcing the catch to come too late in the lift.
- *Putting on the brakes.* When either partner hits the toe picks or skids through the takeoff or flight, the lift is instantly slowed. This means it loses height, flow and ice coverage.

Good

- *High toss.* The higher the lift, the more time there is for rotation.
- *Straight line from takeoff to landing.* This shows that both partners are skating the same pattern.
- *Woman seems weightless.* The lift soars.

History

- The Lutz twist is just one type of twist. Other examples are loop twists, entered like a loop jump, and the Axel twist, based on the Axel jump.
- I remember seeing single Lutz twists in the late 1950s, when they were first introduced by Dafoe and Bowden, but it wasn't until the early sixties that my partner, Guy Revell, and I did the first double twist. We worked on it for months, gradually adding a few more degrees of rotation to the single until at last we had it all the way around—two full rotations! Another thing I remember is that while trying to figure out how to do the extra rotation, I continually slammed the bony part of my left elbow down on the top of Guy's head. His scalp became so bruised that he couldn't comb his hair for weeks!
- Triple twists are now commonplace.

The Death Spiral

The death spiral is one of the most popular moves in pair skating. As the woman arches her back and head toward the ice, she is pulled by the man in a circular path around his center.

Don't confuse the term *spiral* here with the arabesque position performed as a field move. In this instance it refers to the spiraling shape that is etched on the ice by the woman as she curves around her partner.

As their names suggest, the four types of death spiral (forward inside, forward outside, backward inside and backward outside) indicate whether the woman is skating forward or backward and on an inside or an outside edge for the duration of the glide.

Entry

Death spirals often figure prominently in the choreography of a program because they are such a dramatic element and need to be placed well to be highlighted.

Skaters usually skate in a counterclockwise direction in a hand-to-hand position, approaching the element from fast backward crosscuts. As the entry begins, each skater glides on one foot, the man always on a right back outside edge reaching behind with his left toe to prepare for a pivot at the center of the spiral. Depending on the type of death spiral, the woman either stays backward or steps forward on the required edge, at which point she starts the move by deeply bending her skating knee and leaning backward and sideways in the direction of her partner's feet.

Position

The woman only attains this beautifully arched position if she stretches her whole torso up, including her hips. To do so she needs support from her partner. To the naked eye, there appears to be a huge force between skaters, the man pulling into a

DEATH SPIRAL OVERVIEW

On the forward inside death spiral, the man enters backward and the woman forward on an inside edge (1). As the woman starts to bend her skating knee and arch sideways toward her partner's feet, the man begins to pull into the center of the circle (2), reaching behind with his left toe (3) to hit a pivot position (4) with his toe firmly in the ice. The woman's head is close to the ice and her back is arched until she is levered up by the man to exit (5).

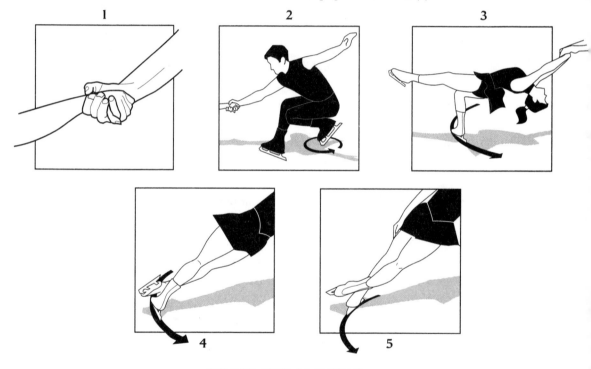

DEATH SPIRAL DETAIL

(1) Many pairs develop unique holds for additional security. In this example, the woman has her hand clasped around the man's baby finger. (2) In full pivot position, the man's weight is strongly over his left toe pick. For the death spiral to be considered "legal," the man must pivot for at least one full rotation. (3) The backward outside death spiral shows the woman skating on a right back outside edge. (4) The backward inside death spiral shows the woman on a left back inside edge. (5) The forward inside death spiral shows the woman skating on a right forward inside edge.

central pivoting point, and the woman pulling in the other direction, away from the center of the circle. Really, the amount of pressure is quite the opposite. It's firm but gentle. If the force was too great, the woman would never be able to reach back far enough with her head toward the ice, or she would flip right off the edge. If the force was too weak, her position would collapse.

Once the woman's head is near the ice, the man is in full pivot position balanced on his left toe pick for at least one entire rotation. Allowing for stylistic factors, if you could draw a line along the woman's free leg and body, down her arm and continue up the man's arm and body, it would form a perfect "V," particularly in the backward outside death spiral.

One critical feature of a good death spiral is that the woman must at all times be skating on a clean edge, without supporting herself with her free hand or with any other part of her body.

Exit

The momentum will decrease as the spiral winds down and as the woman's path reduces the size of her circle. To exit, as the man levers the woman by pulling her up out of the laid-back position, she rolls up out of her arch and swings her free leg around and back to give a little extra boost of speed to finish on a right back outside landing-type edge.

Bad

- *Slow drop into position.* The woman never gets into a completely arched pose due either to lack of knee bend or to not arching from the hips.
- *No speed to end the death spiral.* The edges have been too scratchy on the glides, causing reduced speed.
- *Woman unable to hold clean edge.* The force between the partners is too strong, or not strong enough to provide adequate support.

Good

- *Long duration.* Speed has been maintained and the spiral lasts longer than the required one revolution in pivot position.
- *Woman's head touches the ice.* This shows control and ability to hold the arched posture.

- *Variation in arm or free leg position.* This gives distinction and originality to the move.

History

- The death spiral has long been a pairs component, but it wasn't until 1948 at the World Championships in Davos, Switzerland, that it was first performed in the low position as it is today.
- The backward outside death spiral was the one and only type of death spiral until the seventies, when the forward and backward inside spirals were introduced. The backward outside is still considered the most difficult of all the death spirals.
- The only forward outside death spiral I've ever seen was done by 1993 World champions Isabelle Brasseur and Lloyd Eisler.

The Hip Lift

The hip lift is another type of lift in pair skating that is distinctive because of the woman's position in the air. Using her toe like a pole vault during the takeoff, the woman jumps into an upside-down cartwheel position with one hand pushing down against the man's shoulders.

It's an impressive lift even in its easiest form, and the man's job is fairly simple. The potential for speed and ice coverage without a high danger factor makes it popular among less talented "lifters." You can even do neat and interesting variations without making the lift too challenging.

Preparation

Obviously, the diagonal pattern is a favorite for pair skaters because it provides the greatest amount of ice on which to glide. The hip lift also takes advantage of the corner-to-corner setup, with the couple skating backward hand in hand. The skaters continue moving backward into a hold as they would in a tango dance position, except that instead of putting his right hand around the woman's back, in the hip lift the man rests it on the woman's left hip in order to use the hip as a balance point.

These changes of position sound complex, but a pair team works out the mechanics in shoes on the floor before performing the lift on the ice, so that when they do move onto the ice they can perform the lift relatively easily. It's normal and safer for pair skaters to begin learning a new lift off the ice. The next stage is to try it out on skates at a very slow speed, gradually picking up speed as the lift becomes easier to do.

Takeoff

The launch is initiated as the woman stabs her toe pick in the ice and kicks her other leg up behind in the same way she would kick into a handstand. The man bends under the lift to assist with the jump, straightening his knees as the lift moves upward.

PAIR HIP LIFT OVERVIEW

As in the toe loop, the woman uses the left toe pick like a pole vault to begin flight (1). While the man bends deeply to get under the lift (2), the woman kicks her right leg behind in the same way she would kick into a handstand (3), her left hand pushing down against the man's shoulder. The man balances the woman on her left hip (4) as the lift turns. For the landing, the man lowers the woman to the ice with both hands (5 and 6) and carefully places her on a right back outside edge (7).

PAIR HIP LIFT DETAIL

As the woman is about to pick, the partners move closer and the man places his right hand on the woman's left hip.

The woman kicks into an upside-down cartwheel position, pressing down with her left hand on the man's right shoulder. To make this movement easier, the man bends deeply beneath her.

Once the man's arms are fully extended, the lift rotates easily. With secure balance, the partners may even drop all holds except for the man's right hand on the woman's hip.

Flight

The woman's cartwheel or handstand position allows for numerous leg variations throughout the lift, including the split and the stag; she can also hold her legs straight with her feet crossed. Often the team finds a certain position produces a faster or more stable lift. When they have mastered the basics of a particular lift, the two partners will spend many hours doing research to discover which technique creates the best overall element and what tricks they can add to the lift to make it harder and more appealing to the judges.

If the difficulty of the lift is increased by the man adding rotation, the woman's movement along her overhead path is paused as she centers over the middle axis and spins as a unit with her partner.

Landing

Imagine the aerial path the woman must travel before landing on the right back outside edge as a full half-circle over the man's head.

Bad

- *Sluggish takeoff.* The woman is slow in getting into the cartwheel position, which makes the lift look labored and heavy.
- *Early landing.* The aerial path is incomplete and the lift lands a quarter of a circle too soon.

Good

- *Woman appears weightless.* The lifting technique is so superior that the woman's hands barely touch the man's shoulders.
- *Edges and turns are quiet.* Noiselessness is a good element, indicating speed and comfort.

History

- The hip lift has many names, including the cartwheel and the star lift. Each lift has its own peculiarities and its own specific techniques, and each lift can be tailor-made to suit the particular skills of the skaters.

The Throw Axel

Just watching a throw strikes terror in my heart. Of all the pair tricks, the throws are the most explosive. They are faster, higher, stronger and longer and take more nerve, control and split-second timing than any other element. These are individual solo jumps, which are assisted at takeoff, and named accordingly. For example, there is a throw known as a throw double Axel and another one called a throw triple Sal.

I think it's almost cruel to think that skaters who can't land triple jumps performed solo are expected to land them from a throw, where the power and forces at work are many times greater.

Preparation

Using the diagonal setup, the woman leads the team into the throw from back cross-cuts. While she is settling on the right back outside edge, the man changes places by turning past her to begin the rotational wind-up. In the three common types of throw—the Axel, the Salchow and the toe loop—the man holds the woman around the waist with the right arm, although his grip may vary somewhat depending on the type of throw.

Takeoff

As the woman steps or turns onto her takeoff edge, she springs off her bent knee at the same time as the man pitches her into the air, increasing speed, velocity and height. Now the woman must handle the jump on her own, reaching to its full height to give herself time to rotate.

Flight

Good jumping technique takes over. As long as the pitch has not twisted the woman's body off a vertical axis, she can tuck her arms and legs tightly into spinning position,

PAIR THROW AXEL OVERVIEW

Approaching the takeoff, the partners are "hip to hip" as they glide backward (1 and 2). Both skaters turn forward (3) and the woman pushes onto the left forward outside edge takeoff for the Axel jump (4). As the woman kicks with her right leg, the man throws her into the air (5), adding height, speed and distance to the woman's solo Axel (6–9), which she lands unassisted (10).

PAIR THROW AXEL DETAIL

During the final seconds of the backward preparation, the couple skates hip to hip, with the man's right arm around the woman's back, ready to assist her takeoff with additional power.

To begin the jumping action, both partners turn forward. The woman steps onto the left outside edge for the Axel takeoff.

At the same time as the woman kicks forward to begin flight, the man straightens his bent knees and throws the woman into the air, releasing his grip and spinning her as she moves past him.

holding the rotation for one, two or three revolutions. Only through experience does the skater learn the feeling that tells her when to open up the rotation in preparation for the landing.

While the woman is soaring, take a look at the man. The effort it takes to pitch the woman into the air pulls him off balance for a moment. Of course he's just reacting to the force of the throw, but during that second he's a "stumble bunny," with arms flailing and feet tripping. It's not a pretty sight!

Landing

The force of the throw is so immense that the woman usually lands far away from her partner on the standard back outside edge, a state that I find takes some clever choreography to repair. I don't mind the fact that the skaters are doing totally different things, I just find their separateness too jarring.

Bad

- *The woman under-rotates or over-rotates the jump.* Without a clean landing, a fall is inevitable.
- *Poor pitch.* The timing or rhythm of the partners is out of synch and alters the direction of the throw, which causes the woman to lose her balance in the air.

Good

- *A general feeling of confidence.* A woman's strong and aggressive attitude can make the throw successful.
- *High speed on a long, clean landing.* This shows everything has worked to its potential. When the landing can be held, it emphasizes the good technique.

History

- Skaters talk about two distinct styles of throw: the Russian style, where the man pitches the woman across the ice for distance, and the North American style, where the man pitches the woman up for height.
- 1979 World pair champions Tai Babilonia and Randy Gardner from the United States were the first pair to skate the throw triple Salchow.

Pair Spins

Top-quality pair spins accentuate the creativity of the skaters. Original positions and clever transitions in spins are challenges every team must face in the design of both short and long programs. The progress in the development of these spins mirrors the growing importance of spins in skating generally, and the judges are expecting greater things all the time. It's no longer acceptable to treat the pair spin as a throwaway element.

Preparation

Although both skaters will approach the entrance of the spin in the standard method, the fact that there are two of them creates an unusual situation. To visualize a pair spin preparation, think of the face of a clock in which one skater is at the six o'clock position and the other at midnight; both partners are skating backward in a clockwise direction. Each skater winds up in the standard manner, on the right back inside edge with the left arm in front.

Entry

As the skaters prepare to push forward on the left foot, they imagine a spinning point at the very center of the clock's face and aim to step and turn around that point. Rather than reaching for each other as soon as they pass by the center, they firmly pull their respective spinning circles more tightly until they can smoothly connect into their hold. For pair skaters, the exact center of the spin is actually between the partners instead of down the middle axis of either body.

Position

Look for the same aesthetic standards in pair spins as in singles, but beware! Pair skaters have invented a few spinning positions that are still unnamed.

PAIR CAMEL SPIN OVERVIEW

Picture a clock with a huge face painted on the ice and the partners skating on it clockwise and backward, opposite each other at six o'clock and midnight (1) in the standard spin preparation. When they step forward (2), they circle around each other, grabbing left hands, the man pulling himself around a three-turn (3) until his position is parallel to the woman's (4). To exit the camel, both skaters drop their spiraling leg (5) and push away from the spin (6) on a forward edge.

PAIR CAMEL SPIN

Every pair develops a unique type of handhold that promotes security and safety. Here the woman clasps the man's thumb.

In the most beautiful and fastest pair camels, the woman is tucked tightly under the man. Leg positions, in terms of height, extension and turnout, must match.

During a pair camel spin, the actual center of rotation lies between the two partners. The woman usually skates on a left forward outside edge and the man skates on a left back inside edge.

In pair spins, skaters must spin very close to one another for maximum speed. All it takes to accelerate is for both skaters to pull their upper bodies away from the center of the spin. Maintaining this speed, however, takes consistency in the amount of pressure pulling between partners.

One partner can strategically offset the other partner's weaknesses. For example, if the woman is in a pretzel-like camel, nobody cares what the man is doing because the woman is the focus of the movement. He doesn't necessarily have to be a pretzel, too! His important role is to keep the spin rotating and to help his partner sustain her difficult position without losing speed or center.

Exit

As in single spins, the most common exit is with the woman on the right back outside edge and the man on a left forward outside edge.

Bad

- *Partners aim directly for each other in the entry.* If they crash into one another, the pattern of the entrance has been too straight, and the spin won't rotate with any speed or duration.
- *Unequal pressure between partners.* The spin will lose its center and wobble around the ice. The worst case scenario is that one partner will fall.

Good

- *Smooth position changes.* The spin's speed remains consistent.
- *Imaginative style.* Creative positions make the spin interesting and increase the difficulty.

History

- In spins, no movements are allowed in which the woman is swung around with her feet off the ice. And although spinning lifts in which the man holds the woman by her hand or foot are permitted in the pro ranks, in eligible competition they're strictly forbidden because they are too acrobatic.

Judging: Getting the Facts

A s a young skater in competition, I remember being totally terrified of judges. They all seemed to wear huge galoshes, gaze through coke-bottle lenses and speak in whispers—and I was convinced it was all bad stuff they were saying . . . about me! Rumors were rampant that all judges were on power trips, that you had to behave like a perfect pint-sized adult both on and off the ice if you wanted good marks and that certain judges played favorites. If you weren't one of them, you could forget it! It wouldn't matter what you did, you'd never win.

The sport of figure skating may have progressed by leaps and bounds over the last decade, but our prejudices against judges haven't moved a blade's length.

So who are these judges anyway?

Are judges really a bunch of heartless and ignorant ogres with hidden agendas, or are they a group of people genuinely interested in the advancement of skating who continually suffer from bad press? There are some things you should know before you triple Axel yourself over the boards and into the "It's rigged!" camp.

Judges, many of whom are former competitors, are not plucked randomly off some street corner. It takes years of dedication and training to serve on an international panel. Candidates must pass oral and written examinations, as well as an interview by the International Skating Union. Not only are they required to keep up to date on all the rules, they must participate in regular seminars and receive recommendations from senior officials. And as the last true amateurs in the sport, they don't even get paid for all the grief.

Until recent years, judges were virtually sequestered, never having to defend their marks in public. Now judges are trained to be accountable and credible. They learn to cope with external pressure from the skaters, the fans and the media, and to become skilled in making split-second decisions objectively and independently. Although a judge may face the media with fear and trepidation, I can honestly say I have rarely met one who couldn't defend his mark with valid and thoughtful reasons.

Now that's not to say there haven't been some real judging rhubarbs over the years. In the early days, patriotic marking based on deals between countries was fairly commonplace. Today, particularly at the lower levels, marking a skater based on protocol or reputation is still a temptation for many less-experienced judges. And cultural differences are also a factor. Traditionally, European judges favor a more classical skating style, whereas officials from North America tend to reward the more modern performances.

Controversy is inevitable. With such a complex marking system—and we'll get to that in a moment—it's no surprise fans, skaters and officials may be at opposite ends of the podium. For example, a judge is officially called on the carpet for showing national bias if he favors his own skater, but if he doesn't he's reprimanded at home. He can't win. Part of a judge's job, therefore, is knowing that to some people his decision will always be wrong.

Many of the problems surrounding any judging controversy have been the result of miscommunication. The unwillingness of judges to talk and the media's insatiable appetite for a story have stirred things up. If there's any hint of a fix, the media goes wild. And when you consider how difficult it is to explain the scoring system in simple language, everybody gets suspicious.

Let's tackle the scoring system

Amateur competition is marked on a scale between 0 (not skated) and 6 (perfect and faultless), using decimals to further distinguish between skaters. Each judge gives a skater two marks out of 6.0, the first for technical content and the second for presentation.

In arriving at the technical mark, judges are looking at the overall difficulty of the performance, as well as analyzing the execution of the jumps and spins for singles and the pair moves for pairs and studying the difficulty of the connecting steps and movements for all skaters. Skaters are rewarded for variety, cleanness and precision in their skating, but above all, judges want to see speed.

For the presentation mark, judges consider whether a program is a "harmonious composition" reflecting the mood of the music. The choreography should use the whole ice surface, with a variety of speed and originality. And the skater had better perform with style. Generally speaking, judges want to see the total package: superior athletic ability, charismatic looks and showmanship.

The next time you're watching an event, write down all the judges' marks for both technical merit and presentation. When you're done, look at one judge's marks for all skaters, adding the technical and presentation marks together in each case, instead of looking across the panel at all the marks for one skater. Taking those totals for the whole field, but only one judge at a time, find out which skater earned that particular judge's highest score and assign that skater a 1, for first place. Then find that judge's second-highest score and assign that skater a 2, for second place, and continue on for the rest of the competitors. Those placements, the 1s and 2s, are called ordinals. It's the ordinals that actually determine the outcome, not the value of the points. Here's how.

After going through the totals of every judge for every skater, the results sheet will look like a hodgepodge of ordinals, or placements, depending how each judge viewed the performance of each skater. From a panel of seven judges, let's say skater X got first-place votes from four judges (1×4), two seconds (2×2) and one third (3×1). In the same event, skater Y got three first-place votes (1×3) and four seconds (2×4). Because skater X had the majority of first-place ordinals (4 of a possible 7), skater X wins.

That's why a panel always consists of an odd number of judges, usually 7 or 9 at international events, so that the majority decision rules. With the ordinal system, no one judge can topple the result in one direction or another. If only point values were used, one judge could control the outcome by giving a very high or a very low mark. Not so in figure skating, despite what you may read in the newspapers.

If ordinals are so important, why have points at all?

Having real marks allows the judges to view each performance on a standardized scale. If only ordinals were used, judges would have less range to place the skaters within the field. The chance for error and confusion would be even greater.

For instance, let's say in a field of twenty-four, a judge is marking the seventeenth skater. If we eliminated points and used only ordinals, the judge would have to know exactly where to place that skater despite the fact that there were still more competitors to come. How could any judge rank just one competitor before seeing the whole event?

Under the present system, the judge doesn't need to know exactly where in the field he wants that skater to finish. What he does need to know is the value of that performance on a scale between zero and 6.0, awarding, for example, a technical mark of 4.1 and a presentation mark of 4.7. Using the ordinals from that combined total of 8.8 will determine the placing. In fact, that extra step in the scoring process—

the step from points to ordinals—makes the system even more honest.

Most national and international events require skaters to compete in both short and long (or free) programs. The short program is worth 33.3 percent of the total and the long is worth 66.7 percent. The skater's placement in each program is multiplied by a factor (0.5 for short and 1.0 for long), and at the end of the whole event, those factored placements are added together to determine the champion. The skater with the lowest factored placing wins the event.

To demonstrate, skater X wins the short program, so her first-place finish, 1, is multiplied by 0.5 to reflect the short program's value of 33.3 percent, giving her 0.5 factored placings ($1 \times 0.5 = 0.5$). Skater Y is second in the short, for 1.0 factored placings ($2 \times 0.5 = 1.0$). In the long program, however, skater Y wins with 1.0 factored placings ($1 \times 1.0 = 1.0$), for a combined short and long total of 2.0 factored placings ($1.0 + 1.0 = 2.0$). Skater X, meanwhile, is second in the long program, with 2.0 factored placings ($2 \times 1.0 = 2.0$), for a combined short and long total of 2.5 factored placings ($0.5 + 2.0 = 2.5$). Skater Y wins, therefore, with the lowest factored total.

Skaters around the world have made such enormous advances in their skill level that now tie-breaking rules are often used to determine the winners of the big events. There are such minute differences separating the abilities of the world's top skaters, it's become a nightmare for the judges. Imagine, for instance, having to measure hundredths of a second between runners—but doing it without a clock.

And there can be some preposterous situations.

From the skater's perspective, one gloomy scenario is to select first place to skate. No judge in their right mind will give a high mark to the first skater, particularly if it's a large field. They simply have to leave room for the possibility that other skaters will be better. So here's what happens. You're watching an event. The first skater of a field of twenty-four performs and he's fabulous—but only gets marks in the 5.5 range. The crowd goes into a frenzy, screaming, "6, 6, 6 . . ." That's just dumb. If that first skater is the best of the day, he'll still win, even with a 5.5, but if he isn't and the judges have already given him their 6.0s, what marks do they give skater twelve, who really is the best? They haven't got any marks left.

The bottom line is that skating competitions are like elections. No winner can officially be declared until the last vote for the last skater is in. Everything is in a constant state of flux, with the potential for things to change dramatically up to and including the last competitor. And that's the thrill of it all.

A Comparison of Jump Takeoffs

Jump	edge/toe	direction	edge	takeoff foot*
Axel	edge	F	O	left
Salchow	edge	B	I	left
loop	edge	B	O	right
toe loop	toe	B	O	right
flip	toe	B	I	left
Lutz	toe	B	O	left

*for counterclockwise rotation

F—forward
B—backward

O—outside
I—inside

Index